ideals
EASTER

More Than 50 Years of Celebrating Life's Most Treasured Moments

Vol. 53, No. 2

*"For this day is holy unto our Lord: neither be ye sorry;
for the joy of the Lord is your strength."*

—*Nehemiah 8:10*

IDEALS—Vol. 53, No. 2 March MCMXCVI IDEALS (ISSN 0019-137X) is published eight times a year: February, March, May, June, August, September, November, December by IDEALS PUBLICATIONS INCORPORATED, 535 Metroplex Drive, Suite 250, Nashville, TN 37211. Second-class postage paid at Nashville, Tennessee, and additional mailing offices. Copyright © MCMXCVI by IDEALS PUBLICATIONS INCORPORATED. POSTMASTER: Send address changes to Ideals, PO Box 305300, Nashville, TN 37230. All rights reserved. Title IDEALS registered U.S. Patent Office.

SINGLE ISSUE—U.S. $5.95 USD; Higher in Canada
ONE-YEAR SUBSCRIPTION—8 issues—U.S. $19.95 USD; Canada $36.00 CDN (incl. GST and shipping); Foreign $25.95 USD
TWO-YEAR SUBSCRIPTION—16 issues—U.S. $35.95 USD; Canada $66.50 CDN (incl. GST and shipping); Foreign $47.95 USD

The cover and entire contents of IDEALS are fully protected by copyright and must not be reproduced in any manner whatsoever.

Printed and bound in USA by The Banta Company, Menasha, Wisconsin. Printed on Weyerhaeuser Husky.

The paper used in this publication meets the minimum requirements of
American National Standard for Information Sciences—Permanence of Paper for Printed Library Materials, ANSI Z39.48-1984.

Unsolicited manuscripts will not be returned without a self-addressed, stamped envelope.

ISBN 0-8249-1136-9   GST 131903775

Your privacy is important to us. From time to time we allow other companies, such as book clubs, to mail offers to our subscribers if we think the offer is appropriate. On occasion we also make offers to our subscribers by telephone to purchase Ideals books. If you would prefer not to receive these offers, please let us know by calling 1-800-558-4343 or writing to Customer Service Department, Ideals Publications Inc., P.O. Box 305300, Nashville, TN 37230.

Inside Front Cover
BLUEBIRD AND APPLE BLOSSOMS
Susan Bourdet, artist.
Courtesy of the artist and Wild Wings, Inc.
Lake City, Minnesota

Inside Back Cover
Detail from EBONY AND IVORY
Persis Clayton Weirs, artist.
Courtesy of the artist and Wild Wings, Inc.
Lake City, Minnesota

Cover Photo
BOTANICAL GARDENS
Superstock

Renewal

Virginia Borman Grimmer

Come, fair maiden Springtime,
　　And take me by the hand.
Let me walk through woodlands
　　To where the gentian stand.

Lead me to the pastures
　　That teem with sprouting green,
And show me all the beauty
　　That's starting now to preen.

Also take me farther
　　To a niche where warming sun
Kisses sleeping hyacinths
　　To tell them winter's done.

And lift my weary senses
　　From dreary months just past,
So I can find renewal
　　In wonders sweet and vast.

AZALEAS IN THE WOODS
Martha's Vineyard, Massachusetts
Dianne Dietrich Leis Photography

Marvels of March

Elisabeth Weaver Winstead

March whistles by
with a wild wind song,
Stirring my heart as it trips along.
Nature awakes from an ice-frozen sleep
With a springtime rendezvous to keep
As March in artful, capricious ways
Bursts forth in a swirl of dazzling days.

The pussy willow, waking, is first to stir;
The maple tree casts a smoky-haze blur.
Redbirds call out in the frost-cool breeze
As they fly to welcome tall oak trees.
A shy crocus raises its silvery cup,
Braving the snow as its fair head pops up.

March closes the lock on winter's cold scene
And opens the door to spring's leaves of green.
Bright blooms of forsythia scatter and blow;
The budding white dogwood drops ruffles of snow.
These sparkling mosaics form only a part
Of the marvels of March and amazing spring art.

Readers' Reflections

OPEN MY HEART THAT I MAY SEE

I stood looking out of a window
And complained in my usual way
Of the rain that was steadily falling,
Upsetting my plans for the day.

I didn't know someone had heard me,
So it gave me somewhat of a start
When I heard a quiet voice ask me,
"Have you looked for the sun in your heart?"

Then I saw the little old lady
Whose voice made a path through the gloom,
And the weather outside was forgotten
As her smile seemed to light up the room.

I wondered what power had given
Such strength to a body so frail;
Then I saw she was reading her Bible,
Yes, her Bible—printed in Braille.

John W. Williams
DeWitt, Iowa

THE MORNING

I guess a morning person
Is what I'll always be.
To see the morning sun come up
Quite simply pleases me.

I brew a pot of coffee
As soon as I get up.
It's such a warm and cheerful drink
Served in a pretty cup.

I think of all the things I'll do
Much later in the day;
I sort things out and find that I
Keep organized that way.

I find I'm not the only one
Who likes these morning hours;
The morning-glories all awake
Before the other flowers.

Perhaps they too enjoy the peace
Before the day's begun;
And just like me, they thrill to see
The rising of the sun!

Cherri Turnbull
Albuquerque, New Mexico

FIRST FLIGHT

Today God allowed me to witness
The most beautiful, exciting sight—
Every detail and every movement
Of a baby robin's first flight.

His body was nearly full-grown,
But his legs were spindly and long.
He hopped up and down on the edge of the nest,
Singing a frightened, pitiful song.

His mother came from time to time,
Bringing food and moral support.
But, like a good mother, she didn't push;
And she kept her visits short.

From a nearby tree she called him
In a language only he understood.
You could see him building up courage,
Then he jumped—like I knew he would.

For a while he just stayed on the ground,
Till his wobbly legs could agree.
Then inch by inch I watched him struggle
Up the limb of a mulberry tree.

I could see the pride in that mother
As she coaxed him to try his wings.
I wanted to shout, "I know how you feel!
I watched my son do all the same things.

I know how it feels to want to be near
As long as he needs your help.
But I also know how it feels to step back
And let him fly—by himself."

Mary Horner
Paducah, Kentucky

APRIL GIFT

A capricious April squall
Sweeps along my garden wall,
Replete with scudding cloud,
Bits of sunshine, thunder loud,
Gusting winds, in fits and starts.
A nurturing rain imparts
Alike to field and hills
And to my young daffodils.
This storm's a gift God bestows—
Neatly tied with bright rainbows.

Gene Ash
Lancaster, Ohio

A SONGBIRD

I hear your sweet song as I wake in the morn.
Through my window I see the tree you adorn.
I watch as you gracefully glide through the air
From tree to bush and then over there.
On a branch of the tree, you present a grand sight
With your feathers all preened and colors so bright.
I pause now and listen for more of your song;
But when I look out, I find you have gone.
So tomorrow I'll look out my window to see
If you've come back to perch in my tree
To sing once again your melodious song;
And hopefully then your stay will be long.
But if it's not, then I'll be content
To know that a songbird from heaven was sent.

Gene Wymer
Salamanca, New York

BLOOMING REDBUDS. Missouri. Gay Bumgarner Photography.

Morning Song

Isla Paschal Richardson

A picture is framed by my window. There
Is an artist's goal in that shining square
Displaying white dogwood in zigzag sprays.
Beside it the redbud tree bends and sways

DOGWOOD. Blue Ridge Parkway, North Carolina. Norman Poole Photography.

In the warm south wind. A colorful scene—
    The low crisscross branches above the green
Of the soft spring carpet of velvet grass.
    In robes white and purple they come to mass;
The dogwood and redbud trees lift on high
    Their blossoming boughs to the morning sky.
In beauty and fragrance their voices they raise,
    Offering to God their reverent praise.

LEGENDARY AMERICANS

NANCY SKARMEAS

MARJORIE KINNAN RAWLINGS

Marjorie Kinnan grew up with dreams of becoming a storyteller. Born in 1896, she spent her childhood in Washington, D.C., where at the public schools and in her neighborhood she thrilled the other children with her made-up tales. After high school, Kinnan moved to Madison, Wisconsin, where she enrolled at the University of Wisconsin and became active in the campus dramatic society and continued to work on her writing. After college, her goal remained unchanged; she spent the next decade working for a series of newspapers as a copywriter and feature writer. But through all these years, her attempts at writing and publishing fiction met with disappointment. It was not to be until she was in her early thirties that Kinnan, by then married to Charles

Rawlings and living in north central Florida, realized her dreams. There was something about the large orange grove at Cross Creek where she and her husband made their home and about the character of the people who lived around them that brought Rawlings's artistic vision finally into focus and made her a writer of fiction.

Rawlings and her husband moved to Florida in 1928, just before the onset of the Great Depression. Most of their neighbors lived isolated, harsh lives made only worse by the tough economic times. Theirs was an insular society, mistrustful of outsiders. Rawlings, however, did not remain an outsider for long. She was drawn to the reserved and tough, yet good-humored, character of her new neighbors; and she immersed herself in their lives and customs. Although she met with suspicion from many, Rawlings was not to be discouraged. The woman who had dreamed all her life of being a writer had found the subject that made her imagination and her pen come alive. Within two years, Rawlings sold her first two short stories, both tales from rural north-central Florida, to *Scribner's Magazine*. Unfortunately, Rawlings's husband did not share her commitment to Florida's rugged backcountry; as she immersed herself in life at Cross Creek, he continued to distance himself from it and from her. Shortly after the publication of Rawlings's first novel in 1933, she and her husband were divorced. From that point on, Cross Creek was hers alone.

Throughout the thirties, Rawlings continued to write and publish short stories to critical acclaim. In 1938, she caught the attention of all of America with her novel, *The Yearling*, which won the 1939 Pulitzer Prize for fiction. The moving but unsentimental story of a young Florida boy and an orphaned fawn, *The Yearling* sold more than 500,000 copies in twenty-one printings in its first year alone and was translated worldwide. Only three years later, Rawlings became the talk of the literary community once more with the publication of *Cross Creek*, a collection of autobiographical vignettes about her life at her Florida orange-grove home. *Cross Creek* is fact and experience blended wonderfully with touches of fiction. It is, in Rawlings own words, the story of her "life in the woods"; but in truth it is much more—a tribute to a time and a place and a way of life, and a record of one woman's thoughtful journey of self-discovery. Rawlings did not merely use Cross Creek for inspiration for her writing; she worked hard to make a life for herself there, and she succeeded.

In 1941, Rawlings married for the second time. Her new husband, Norton Sanford Baskin, was an old friend from St. Augustine, Florida. The couple resided in St. Augustine for a time and then later bought an old farmhouse in upstate New York, which became Rawlings's summer home. Only a few years after their marriage, at the height of her popularity as a writer, Rawlings put her creative work on hold while she served the Allies during World War II. She sold war bonds, worked for civil defense, and used her name and celebrity to appeal to the American people to support the war effort. She also agreed to reissue *The Yearling* and *Cross Creek* in what were called Armed Service Editions—inexpensive reprints to be distributed to American men and women in service. As a result, Rawlings gained a broad new audience and also received a flood of mail from service people. The author is said to have answered each letter personally, leaving herself little time for writing fiction.

Wartime also brought Rawlings a great personal burden. Her husband, who had volunteered for the American Field Service as an ambulance driver in India and Burma, was for a time believed missing in action. When he was eventually found, he was seriously ill; and his recovery a half a world away became his wife's consuming concern. In all, the war years took a great toll on Marjorie Rawlings. She was in ill health for much of the remainder of her life, although she continued to write until her death in 1953.

Like all great writers, Rawlings was able to reveal the universal behind her specific subject while at the same time portraying the lives and emotions of her characters in wonderful detail and with great honesty. Her true subject, most often, was the human spirit struggling against the burdens of life—whether it was a poor Florida farm couple or a young child coming of age. Rawlings turned fact into fiction without losing any of the authenticity, and she wrote of coarse and bleak lives without neglecting the humor and hope. Her *Cross Creek* has been compared by some to Thoreau's *Walden*, and *The Yearling* is a true classic in literature for children. Margaret Mitchell, author of *Gone with the Wind*, called Rawlings the "born perfect storyteller." It is this legacy that fits her best; Marjorie Rawlings grew up looking for a story to tell. She found it far from her childhood home in the woods and farms and orange groves of Florida. Although her years at Cross Creek were only one short interlude in her life, they were her defining experience. It was at Cross Creek, as she struggled to make a life for herself alone in a harsh and unfamiliar environment, that Marjorie Rawlings became the storyteller she had dreamed all her life of being.

Nancy Skarmeas is a book editor who enjoys knitting, running, and playing with her dalmations, Lucy and Riley, at her home in New Hampshire. Her Greek and Irish ancestry has fostered a lifelong interest in research and history.

Days of Spring

Gertrude Dicks

Lace of green the hills are wearing
On this sunny springtime day,
And the meadow grass is scheming
To become sweet summer hay.

Yellow ribbons in profusion
Hug each lilting, laughing rill
While the melodies in concert
Leave no songbirds mute or still.

I suppose of all the seasons
This one earns the best of prose,
But who needs a rhyme or reason
When Spring walks on satin toes?

Song of the Wood

LaVerne P. Larson

The lace-edged dawn with rosy glow
　　Weaves ropes of golden light
As darkness spreads its velvet wings
　　And silently takes flight.

The woodland trails begin to sing
　　Sweet magic melodies
As nature stirs and slowly wakes
　　Mid soft and gentle breeze.

The brown earth, rich and warm again,
　　Grows green with promise fair;
A sweet perfume of earth and wood
　　Floats on the balmy air.

Each woodland creature, bright-eyed now
　　From winter's quiet rest,
Playfully scampers to and fro,
　　Filled with springtime zest.

The sun's rays kiss the woodland trails
　　As does the silver rain;
And when a rainbow bridge appears,
　　All earth is bright again.

Beauty, peace, and happiness
　　Dwell o'er the woodland sod;
For all the trails are tended
　　By the gentle hands of God.

RHODODENDRON PETALS
Blue Ridge Parkway, North Carolina
Norman Poole Photography

Laura K. Griffis

CASTILLO DE SAN MARCOS. Photograph courtesy of St. Augustine and St. Johns County Chamber of Commerce.

THE CASTILLO DE SAN MARCOS
St. Augustine, Florida

A warm Florida breeze blows gently against my face, and I take a deep breath of the salty ocean air. Above me a sea gull circles, stretching his gray-tipped wings against a backdrop of blue sky. From his lofty vantage point he can see what I have come to explore. Soaring above the towering fortress walls, he gazes down on the Castillo de San Marcos.

During its three-hundred year history, the Castillo de San Marcos has wrapped its protective arms around Spanish settlers, British redcoats, Confederate soldiers, and curious tourists. The Castillo stands guard over one of the oldest European settlements in the United States—St. Augustine, Florida. Decades before Pilgrims and Jamestown colonists landed in the New World, Spanish settlers founded

this town and formed a crucial link between Spain and its far-reaching empire.

Pirates and other enemies lurked off the coast, waiting to intercept ships carrying gold and other treasures back to Spain. The original wooden fortress at St. Augustine fell easy prey to pirates. During raids, pirates would loot the town and take colonists prisoner, later holding them for ransom. Spain finally decided that a stronger fortress was needed to protect the vulnerable settlement and ensure that enemies would never again penetrate the fort at St. Augustine.

A Spanish coat of arms chiseled above the entrance pays tribute to the monarchy that began building the new fortress in 1672. Laborers, stone masons, and innovative engineers worked on the fort for years. They made use of one of Florida's natural resources—billions of coquina shells that form a hard rock. Coquina pits on a nearby island provided the countless bricks needed for the Castillo. Over the centuries, these durable blocks have withstood everything from cannonballs to raging hurricanes. Completed in 1695, the Castillo is just over three hundred years old, older than America herself.

The Castillo stretches longer than a football field. Crossing the moat that surrounds the massive, weathered walls, I cannot help but think of the alligators that have inhabited Florida for years. The placid water looks safe, however; and I venture across the moat, approaching the antique drawbridge and the tarnished cannons that bid an ominous welcome.

I feel transported back in time as I leave the warm Florida sunshine and enter the cool darkness of a passageway leading to the fortress's courtyard. The high coquina walls surround me on all four sides. I can picture scores of colonists huddled together in this courtyard, taking refuge in the Castillo during a siege. As their homes were burned and looted, they slept in makeshift tents within the safe walls of the fortress. The fortified walls and booming canons protected colonists from defeat. Even their dogs and chickens found a safe spot in the Castillo.

During a siege, several hundred colonists and soldiers would live off the food kept in large storage rooms that faced the courtyard. They ate dried beans, rice, and corn to survive. Other storage rooms housed weapons and gunpowder.

Throughout times of war and peace, soldiers and colonists gathered in the Castillo's small chapel to pray. St. Augustine represents one of the first Christian outposts in the United States, and religion was an important part of the Spanish settlers' daily lives. I pause at the quiet alcove where many colonists came in search of serenity.

CASTILLO DE SAN MARCOS, FRONT VIEW.
Photograph courtesy of St. Augustine and St. Johns County Chamber of Commerce.

Serenity, however, was a rare visitor to the Castillo. After climbing the stairs to the fort's upper level, I tour the square-shaped deck that provided a place for soldiers to man the cannons during battle. At each of the four corners, a lookout tower served to warn of enemy attack. From this vantage point, Spanish guards could spot pirate ships or British naval vessels as they menacingly neared the shore.

Throughout its tumultuous history, the legendary Castillo has changed hands several times. While the fort never suffered defeat in battle, it was a bargaining chip between Spanish and British monarchs during the fight for control of the New World. In 1821, Spain sold Florida, along with the Castillo de San Marcos, to the United States. The flag of a young American nation, displaying only twenty-three stars, was hoisted above the fortress. Years later, the fort became a battleground for Union and Confederate soldiers during the Civil War. The battles are now over, and today the Castillo de San Marcos peacefully offers its remarkable history to curious tourists such as I.

Standing near one of the lookout towers, I watch the ocean glisten under the Florida sun. I lean against the weathered coquina walls and think about the three centuries of Spanish, British, and American heritage they represent. The fortress reminds me of a medieval castle, strangely out of place among the Florida palm trees. The Castillo de San Marcos seems to belong to another continent and another time, and I realize why it is one of America's most unique historic sites.

A native of Texas, Laura K. Griffis is finishing her senior year at Vanderbilt University while working as an Ideals editorial intern. Laura collects postcards from her travels to museums around the world as a part of her ongoing study of international cultures.

The Nestlings

Grace Tall

Dear Lord who made
The earth and sky,
Without whose nod
No sparrows fly,
Protect the nestlings
In the tree
That shades the house
That shelters me.
Let no wild winds
The young birds harm
Or thundering skies
Cause them alarm.
And in the brief
Rehearsing time
It takes small wings
To learn to climb,
Contrive, dear Lord,
Some way to keep
All dogs indoors,
All cats asleep.

BITS & PIECES

When Jesus hung upon the cross
The birds, 'tis said, bewailed the loss
Of Him who first to mortals taught,
Guiding with love the life of all,
And heeding e'en the sparrow's fall.
　　　　—*Charles Godfrey Leland*

Listen, sweet dove, unto my song
　　And spread thy golden wings on me;
Hatching my tender heart so long,
　　Till it get wing, and fly away with thee.
　　　　—*George Herbert*

There the thrushes
Sing till latest sunlight flushes
In the west.
　　　　—*Christina Rossetti*

What, is the jay more precious than the lark,
Because his feathers are more beautiful?
　　　　—*William Shakespeare*

The nightingale appeared the first;
　And as her melody she sang,
The apple into blossom burst,
　To life the grass and violets sprang.
　　　　　—Henrich Heine

Hear how the birds, on ev'ry blooming spray,
　With joyous music wake the dawning day!
　　　　　—Alexander Pope

Hear the lark begin his flight
And singing startle the dull Night
From his watchtower in the skies
Till the dappled dawn doth rise.
　　　　　—John Milton

Then , little bird, this boon confer;
　Come, and my requiem sing,
Nor fail to be the harbinger
　Of everlasting spring.
　　　　　—William Wordsworth

They'll come again to the apple tree—
　Robin and all the rest—
When the orchard branches are fair to see
　In the snow of the blossoms dressed,
And the prettiest thing in the world will be
　The building of the nest.
　　　　　—Margaret E. Sangster

REBIRTH

Two springtimes ago, I didn't touch the Easter eggs I found. They were the sky blue eggs of a pair of robins. An upstairs window ledge in my home held the nest that the two birds had so carefully cemented with mud and straw.

As the eggs hatched, I had a firsthand view. The young grew and feathered under the watchful care of their parents. At last they tried their wings and ventured out into a new world of sun to become an Easter carol in some future spring.

Last year, I awoke on Easter morning just as the darkness of night was beginning to ease. As the first few pink rays of the sun started to appear in the eastern skies, robins were ushering in the day with their songs and carols. Their joyous chords seemed so appropriate for a sunrise service. It was a devout moment in the dawn before the sun.

As the robins' first rich strains filled the morning hour, how inspiring it was to be a part of that day. It was Easter in all its glory. As I listened, I knew I was alive and that all was well.

The birdsongs celebrated the birth of a new day and a new season. Blossoms spilled their fragrance and hues of loveliness in the flower beds, throughout the woods, and by the roadsides. The grass was green with spring. New leaves were coming, and a new family of blue eggs graced the nest beneath my window.

Here was the beginning, the rebirth, the renewal. And I was a witness to this miracle as robins sang their hymns of glorification.

The author of two published books, Lansing Christman has been contributing to Ideals *for over twenty years. Mr. Christman has also been published in several American, foreign, and braille anthologies. He lives in rural South Carolina.*

Memento

Doris K. Gayzagian

When first we came
To this suburban spot,
My neighbor,
Cleaning out our bordering brook,
Called, "Come,
Take these violets
Before the thistles and long grass
Completely choke them out."

I did.
And now,
Where once bloomed only purple ones,
The strains combined.
Pale petals, lavender and white
With spots and streaks, some dark, some light,
Salute each spring
And gently sing
Their mingled toast to friendship.

VIOLA CORNUTA "CUTY"
R. Todd Davis Photography

April

Gladys Taber

Now the light lengthens as the season moves toward May. Dusk is violet, night cool and tender. Sunrise is luminous. Daffodils star the hill by the pond and bloom in the quiet garden. Violets begin to open their pointed buds. We have the tiny white violets in the meadow, and the dark purple around the house, and the Confederate violets carpeting the border. The Confederate violets are ivory-white streaked with true blue. And by the pond, the yellow dogtooth violets hang their delicate trumpets.

At night, the peepers sing away in the swamp, a flutelike sound. This is the beginning of a new cycle of growth, a quickening of the earth which will only end as the harvest is gathered in the autumn.

When I go out with the dogs, I feel a quickening in my spirit too. The season of bloom is upon us, and then the green summer days, and at last the ripeness of autumn, all ordered and unchanged by the world's dissensions. It is something to count on.

Humbly I thank God for the eternal miracle of spring.

DAME'S VIOLET
Hesperis matronalis
Kewaunee County, Wisconsin
Darryl R. Beers Photography

HANDMADE HEIRLOOM

◆ ◆ ◆

HATBOX HEIRLOOMS. Bruce Curtis Photography.

DECORATED HATBOXES

Mary Skarmeas

When I was a child, people wore hats. On spring afternoons my father would don his straw boater, and we'd ride the subway to Fenway Park in Boston to take in a baseball game. In the stands, I'd look out upon a sea of identical cream-colored straw hats, just like my dad's, covering the head of every man in attendance. Hats were part of the American uniform of daily life. Men wore straw hats in summer and felt hats in the colder months. Although women often saved their favorite hat for Easter Sunday, they topped their heads year-round with every size, shape, and style available. And for every hat, there was a hatbox. These round cardboard boxes with string handles were a common sight along the busy shopping thoroughfares of American cities in the thirties, forties, and fifties. Made of sturdy cardboard to protect the hat inside, extra hatboxes were put to use at home much like shoeboxes today—to store letters, scarves, keepsakes, small children's toys, and anything else that needed its own special place.

Today, hats are the exception, not the rule, in

fashion; and hatboxes are seen more often in antique shops than on people's dressers at home. But hatboxes still have a nostalgic lure for those of us, like me, who remember the days when hats were a fashion standard. They can still protect our cherished items with style and evoke special memories, especially when they are personalized for a momentous occasion. Hatboxes can be decorated with cherished items of sentimental value, such as scraps of lace from a wedding gown and dried flowers from a bride's bouquet. The result is a unique heirloom that might be used to store treasured wedding snapshots and other memorabilia.

Many of us have old hatboxes saved in the attic from years gone by or maybe still use a few to store a special collection or a stack of love letters. Antique shops are also good bets for authentic old hatboxes, which through the years were made in as many shapes and sizes as were the hats they held. But if all else fails, today's modern craft stores can supply hatboxes—maybe not authentic antiques, but perfectly suited for craftwork. You can take a cardboard hatbox, either weathered from years of life or brand new from the craft store, and transform it into a beautiful, functional container customized for a special person or to commemorate a special occasion.

To create a custom gift for a new bride, for example, use white silk fabric and flowers to cover a large hatbox—the perfect place to protect a cherished bouquet or veil. For a baby shower gift, visit a wallpaper store for a pattern to complement the new nursery. You can use crib sheets for lining and tie tiny rattles or stuffed animals on top for a special touch. Inside can go a selection of soft cotton baby clothes, a warm woolen blanket, or a hand-knit sweater. Also, these decorated boxes can be dressed up for a christening gift—covered with white on white paper and accented with satin and lace. You could even attach the birth announcement to the lid. Suggest to the recipient that the box would make the perfect storage place for the christening gown. What a great way to start a tradition and preserve memories.

The process of creating a custom hatbox is relatively simple. The first step is to choose your materials. The next step is to cover the entire exterior of the box with wallpaper or fabric. Cut a strip of your chosen material that is one inch longer than the circumference of the box and two inches wider than the box's depth to allow an overlap at the top and bottom. Using a glue stick, secure the fabric or paper smoothly around the box. When dry, make small vertical clips at even intervals on the overlaps at top and bottom. Fold the extra material neatly down against the inside of the box and flat against the bottom, securing again with the glue stick. Next, trace the bottom of the box on the paper or fabric. Cut this piece and glue it to the outside bottom of the box so that it covers the folded-over edge and creates a neat, finished look. To cover the lid, cut two pieces: one round piece using the lid as a guide, and one strip an inch longer than the circumference of the lid and one half inch wider than the depth of the lid. Glue the strip around the lid. Fold and secure the edges as you did for the body of the box. Next, glue the circle on the top of the lid. If you would like to line the interior of the box, you can use the same fabric or wallpaper, or you can choose a different material for variety.

The basic method of covering can be adapted to whatever occasion and whatever materials you have. Add wallpaper borders over the basic covering for an interesting look, or trim with ribbon and cord. Handles, an update on the old-fashioned string handles used by shoppers to carry their hatboxes home, can be made using lengths of ribbon attached through holes punched in the box's sides. These ribbon handles, tied in a bow, will also secure the cover to the box.

The beauty of these decorated hatboxes is that they are truly an item that every person needs—a unique place to store treasured belongings—and they are ready to be suited to any occasion. Old-fashioned hatboxes dressed up for a special occasion are beautiful, they are practical, and they come complete with their own air of nostalgia, ready to become a treasured heirloom. And for those of us old enough to remember when hats were a part of our everyday dress, they are a sweet reminder of a time when everyone needed a place to store a favorite Easter bonnet.

Mary Skarmeas lives in Danvers, Massachusetts, and is studying for her bachelor's degree in English at Suffolk University. Mother of four and grandmother of one, Mary loves all crafts, especially knitting.

Music
for a Sunday
Afternoon

Roy G. Rogers

Far in the distance I heard the sound,
The thunder tympanic from sky to ground,
Nearer and nearer across the plain—
The boisterous prelude before the rain.

The lightning set the sky ablaze,
Announcing each new, dramatic phrase
With strong staccato from cloud to cloud,
Repeating the rhythm in accents loud.

When at last the prelude's beats were o'er,
The Maestro's baton requested more.
The symphony responded once again
With harmonics of heaven's refreshing rain.

From my orchestra seat on the earth's broad plain
Where the echoes repeated the last refrain,
I thought, as I gazed from the east to the west,
What a beautiful hymn for this day of rest.

LIGHTNING STORM. Kossuth County, Iowa. Ed Harp/Unicorn Stock Photos.

THROUGH MY WINDOW

Pamela Kennedy
Art by Russ Flint

A SUNRISE SERVICE

One of the advantages of marriage to a military man is the opportunity to move from place to place. In twenty-six years of Navy life together, we have moved seventeen times and enjoyed the customs and scenery of many different locales. We've spent Christmas in the snowy northeastern United States as well as in the desert climate of the Southwest. We've enjoyed Thanksgiving feasts near Plymouth Rock and at a Hawaiian beach made of lava from a still active volcano. But one of the most unusual holiday celebrations I've experienced was an Easter sunrise service conducted on the flight deck of the USS *Essex*, a helicopter carrier passing through Pearl Harbor on its way back to San Diego, California.

It seemed an unlikely place to celebrate the Resurrection, a scene I always associate with a quiet garden shrouded in early morning mist. As we walked along the pier where the *Essex* was moored, I heard the rumble and whir of engines, the creak of taut lines straining. I was dwarfed by the huge superstructure as deck after deck of battle gray towered above us. We climbed two flights of metal stairs (ladders in Navy jargon) and crossed the ramp bridging the space between pier and ship. Serious young men in crisp, white uniforms greeted us with salutes and welcomed us aboard. As a small group gathered on the quarter-deck, an escort came to lead us to the flight deck for the services. We wound our way like obedient sheep through mazes of equipment, passage-ways, ladders, and ramps until we eventually emerged on the flight deck—a vast gray plat-form at the stern of the ship. On one side of the deck a half dozen battle-ready helicopters were lashed down with inch-thick cables, a menac-ing venue in which to celebrate the bright hope of Easter morning.

Above us, dark, threatening clouds piled upon one another. The wind whipped across the deck ferociously, knocking over carefully placed Easter lilies, music stands, and metal folding chairs; tearing at flags and skirts and pantlegs. A balding Marine sergeant fiddled with a tape recorder, connecting and discon-necting wires, turning dials, inserting and eject-ing cassettes. What a scene! I wondered who had decided this would be a good idea. Then I felt a few drops of rain. How could anyone be expected to worship under such conditions?

The static crackle of electricity through the amplifier signaled the sergeant had apparently made the right connections. After a few more pops and screeches, his deep voice interrupted my troubled meditation on wind and rain and quiet Easters past. He welcomed us to the *Essex*, then began to sing in a rich baritone that wrapped itself around the deck in the dark morning. His words reminded us of the solemn march of Mary Magdalene on Easter morning, of her despair and fears, her misun-derstandings, her grief. I looked up at the gloomy clouds towering over the mountains and wondered about Mary's doubts that must have piled one upon the other. Then the key changed, and he sang of the unexpected joy she found at the feet of her resurrected Lord as He spoke her name and she realized new hope. There was a murmur in the small congregation gathered on the flight deck, and a little girl pointed to the eastern sky. Thick and golden against the shades of black and gray, wide swaths of sunlight radiated from the broken clouds, falling on the mountains and the wind-whipped water of the harbor. Whitecaps flashed in the streaming light; and we all sat motionless, hushed by the scene before us.

After a few moments, I looked around the flight deck again. We sat on the deck of one of the Navy's most powerful vessels, surrounded by monuments to military technology, yet we were speechless before the magnificence of God's creation. The men and women in this congregation had dedicated themselves to fight their country's battles using all the weapons at their disposal, yet the morning's display of natural beauty said more about the triumph of light over darkness, of good over evil than all the warships and planes humans would ever create. I realized that Easter was not so much about peace and quiet as it was about war. Somehow this ship now seemed a perfect place to celebrate the Resurrection; a perfect place to recall that the ultimate battle of life and death was not fought in a dewy gar-den, but in the dirt and dust of the everyday world. And it was also a perfect place to remember that we need not fear defeat, for the victory has already been secured by our heav-enly Captain.

Pamela Kennedy is a freelance writer of short sto-ries, articles, essays, and children's books. Wife of a naval officer and mother of three children, she has made her home on both United States coasts and currently resides in Honolulu, Hawaii. She draws her material from her own experiences and memo-ries, adding highlights from her imagination to enhance the story.

Denial

Marcia Krugh Leaser

Tired eyes
    searched anxiously
        as shadows came alive.

Loneliness he could not bear
    caused hands to clench tightly
        at his sides.

Inward pain
    tore him apart.
        Angry voices rose and fell.

Fear engulfed his very soul;
    who was left there
        who would tell?

Regardless of
    the promise past
        sworn with impulsive pride.

"I knew Him not."

The rooster crowed;
    then Peter knelt
        and cried.

PETER'S BETRAYAL
St. James
St. Louis, Missouri
Gene Plaisted, OSC
The Crosiers

The Entry

and when they drew nigh unto Jerusalem, and were come to Bethphage, unto the mount of Olives, then sent Jesus two disciples, Saying unto them, Go into the village over against you, and straightway ye shall find an ass tied, and a colt with her: loose them, and bring them unto me. And if any man say ought unto you, ye shall say, The Lord hath need of them; and straightway he will send them.

All this was done, that it might be fulfilled which was spoken by the prophet, saying, Tell ye the daughter of Sion, Behold, thy King cometh unto thee, meek, and sitting upon an ass, and a colt the foal of an ass.

And the disciples went, and did as Jesus commanded them, And brought the ass, and the colt, and put on them their clothes, and they set him thereon. And a very great multitude spread their garments in the way; others cut down branches from the trees, and strawed them in the way.

And the multitudes that went before, and that followed, cried, saying, Hosanna to the son of David: Blessed is he that cometh in the name of the Lord; Hosanna in the highest.

And when he was come into Jerusalem, all the city was moved, saying, Who is this? And the multitude said, This is Jesus the prophet of Nazareth of Galilee.

MATTHEW 21:1-11

THE TRIUMPHANT ENTRY
Detail from Armadio degli Argenti
School of Fra Angelico (1387-1455)
Museo di San Marco, Florence, Italy
Scala/Art Resource, New York

The Last Supper

**a**nd the first day of unleavened bread, when they killed the passover, his disciples said unto him, Where wilt thou that we go and prepare that thou mayest eat the passover?

And he sendeth forth two of his disciples, and saith unto them, Go ye into the city, and there shall meet you a man bearing a pitcher of water: follow him. And wheresoever he shall go in, say ye to the goodman of the house, The Master saith, Where is the guestchamber, where I shall eat the passover with my disciples? And he will shew you a large upper room furnished and prepared: there make ready for us.

And his disciples went forth, and came into the city, and found as he had said unto them: and they made ready the passover.

And in the evening he cometh with the twelve. And as they did eat, Jesus took bread, and blessed, and brake it, and gave to them, and said, Take, eat: this is my body.

And he took the cup, and when he had given thanks, he gave it to them: and they all drank of it. And he said unto them, This is my blood of the new testament, which is shed for many. Verily I say unto you, I will drink no more of the fruit of the vine, until that day that I drink it new in the kingdom of God.

MARK 14:12-17; 22-25

THE LAST SUPPER
Detail from Armadio degli Argenti
School of Fra Angelico (1387-1455)
Museo di San Marco, Florence, Italy
Scala/Art Resource, New York

The Betrayal

and while he yet spake, lo, Judas, one of the twelve, came, and with him a great multitude with swords and staves, from the chief priests and elders of the people.

Now he that betrayed him gave them a sign, saying, Whomsoever I shall kiss, that same is he: hold him fast.

And forthwith he came to Jesus, and said, Hail, master; and kissed him.

And Jesus said unto him, Friend, wherefore art thou come? Then came they, and laid hands on Jesus, and took him.

And, behold, one of them which were with Jesus stretched out his hand, and drew his sword, and struck a servant of the high priest's, and smote off his ear.

Then said Jesus unto him, Put up again thy sword into his place: for all they that take the sword shall perish with the sword.

MATTHEW 26:47-52

THE BETRAYAL
Detail from Armadio degli Argenti
School of Fra Angelico (1387-1455)
Museo di San Marco, Florence, Italy
Scala/Art Resource, New York

The Trial

hen Pilate entered into the judgment hall again, and called Jesus, and said unto him, Art thou the King of the Jews?

Jesus answered him, Sayest thou this thing of thyself, or did others tell it thee of me?

Pilate answered, Am I a Jew? Thine own nation and the chief priests have delivered thee unto me: what hast thou done?

Jesus answered, My kingdom is not of this world: if my kingdom were of this world, then would my servants fight, that I should not be delivered to the Jews: but now is my kingdom not from hence.

Pilate therefore said unto him, Art thou a king then? Jesus answered, Thou sayest that I am a king. To this end was I born, and for this cause came I into the world, that I should bear witness unto the truth. Every one that is of the truth heareth my voice.

Then Pilate therefore took Jesus, and scourged him. And the soldiers platted a crown of thorns, and put it on his head, and they put on him a purple robe, And said, Hail, King of the Jews! and they smote him with their hands.

Then came Jesus forth, wearing the crown of thorns, and the purple robe. And Pilate saith unto them, Behold the man!

When the chief priests therefore and officers saw him, they cried out, saying, Crucify him, crucify him.

JOHN 18:33-37; 19:1-3; 5-6A

THE TRIAL
Detail from Armadio degli Argenti
School of Fra Angelico (1387-1455)
Museo di San Marco, Florence, Italy
Scala/Art Resource, New York

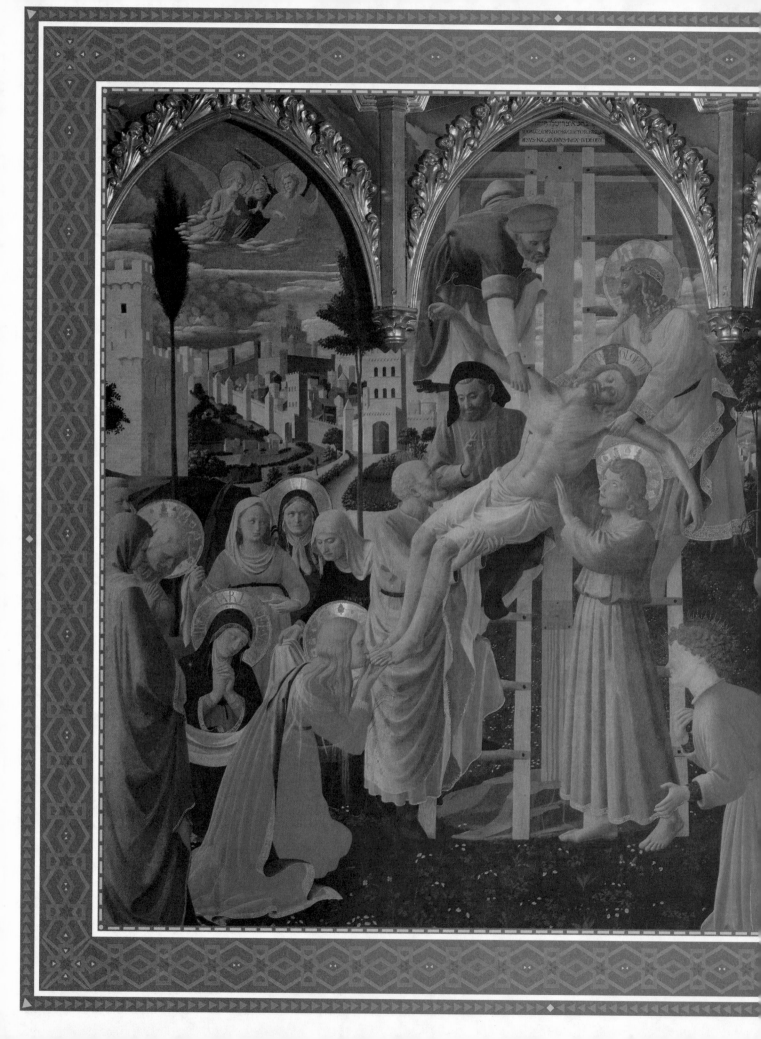

The Son of God

nd Jesus cried with a loud voice, and gave up the ghost. And the vail of the temple was rent in twain from the top to the bottom.

And when the centurion, which stood over against him, saw that he so cried out, and gave up the ghost, he said, Truly this man was the Son of God.

There were also women looking on afar off: among whom was Mary Magdalene, and Mary the mother of James the less and of Joses, and Salome;

And now when the even was come, because it was the preparation, that is, the day before the sabbath, Joseph of Arimathaea, an honourable counsellor, which also waited for the kingdom of God, came, and went in boldly unto Pilate, and craved the body of Jesus.

And Pilate marvelled if he were already dead: and calling unto him the centurion, he asked him whether he had been any while dead. And when he knew it of the centurion, he gave the body to Joseph.

And he bought fine linen, and took him down, and wrapped him in the linen, and laid him in a sepulchre which was hewn out of a rock, and rolled a stone unto the door of the sepulchre.

MARK 15:37-40; 42-46

DEPOSITION
Fra Angelico (1387-1455)
Museo di San Marco, Florence, Italy
Erich Lessing/Art Resource, New York

The Ascension

**a**nd he said unto them, These are the words which I spake unto you, while I was yet with you, that all things must be fulfilled, which were written in the law of Moses, and in the prophets, and in the psalms, concerning me.

Then opened he their understanding, that they might understand the scriptures,

And said unto them, Thus it is written, and thus it behoved Christ to suffer, and to rise from the dead the third day: And ye are witnesses of these things.

And he led them out as far as to Bethany, and he lifted up his hands, and blessed them. And it came to pass, while he blessed them, he was parted from them, and carried up into heaven.

And they worshipped him, and returned to Jerusalem with great joy: And were continually in the temple, praising and blessing God. Amen.

LUKE 24:44-46; 48; 50-53

Mary at the Tomb

Kay Hoffman

She came with burial spices
    While the heavens yet were gray.
Heart filled with grief, she pondered
    Who would roll the stone away.

But lo, the tomb was open;
    The great stone was set aside.
With fearful heart, Mary stooped
    And tried to peer inside.

"Why seekest thou the living
    Here among the dead?"

She heard the angel say.
    "He has risen as He said."

When Mary saw her blessed Lord
    Within the garden fair,
Her heart was filled with rapture
    As she knelt and worshiped there.

The words He spoke to Mary
    He still speaks to us today:
"Go tell the others that I live."
    The stone is rolled away.

Christ Is Alive!

Beverly J. Anderson

Rejoice! Rejoice! It's Easter Day;
The angels rolled the stone away.
Christ conquered death and sin and strife
To give to us eternal life.

Triumphantly the church bells ring:
"Christ is alive—our risen King!"
Oh, blessed assurance, saving grace,
One day we'll see Him face to face.

Today the message shines anew,
Its aged promise ever true.
How can a soul be sad, I say;
For hope was born on Easter Day.

Rejoice! Rejoice! Be glad of heart
For all that Easter doth impart.
Christ is alive! Oh, let us sing
Hosannas to our risen King!

An Easter Offering

Nancy S. Boston

Now, Nature, from the fertile mold
Your store of treasure vast unfold;
And from your warm and pulsing heart
New life once more to earth impart.
O'er hill and vale and meadow wide,
On mountain lone, by ebbing tide
Unfold the buds of promise sweet,
The waiting world again to greet;
And resurrect the flowers fair—
A perfumed incense on the air.
And this, a humble tribute, bring,
Earth's offering to her Easter King.

Let Nature's minstrelsy awake!
The gentle wind love's message take
In music's notes of sweetest strain
Till flowing brooks catch the refrain
And murm'ring gently to the sea
Repeat the song from lea to lea.
Then wake the ocean's mighty soul,
And o'er its billows anthems roll.
Let woodland carolers be heard
And chant again the joyous word;
From cliff to cliff Te Deums ring
Hosanna to the Saviour King!

Oh, lives with these great blessings fraught,
A gift of love divinely bought,
To Him who hath our ransom paid,
The hope of joy eternal made,
Let grateful hearts their homage pay
And give Him praise from day to day;
Till round the world we will proclaim
The glories of the Saviour's name;
And in an endless anthem sing,
He lives, our resurrected King!

PEAR ORCHARD
Hood River Valley, Oregon
Steve Terrill Photography

A Tribute to Springtime

Until

Ardis Rittenhouse

I like to look at lots of green—
     Not just the kind you find on bills
But what you find in meadows full
     Of dandelions and daffodils,
The kind that comes up in the spring
     So lush in sunshine's warming glow.
I really like that springtime grass—
     Until it's tall enough to mow!

God, grant that I may never be
A scoffer at eternity
As long as every April brings
     The sweet rebirth of growing things.

—Sara Henderson Hay

Spring hangs her infant blossoms
     on the trees,
Rocked in the cradle
     of the western breeze.

—William Cowper

Come Gently, Spring

Ethel H. Bruce

I would not ask that Spring's return
Be well defined; I love the way
Springtime arrives by small degrees,
How hills grow greener day by day
And buds swell on the willow tree.

One crocus bloom can set the heart
Awhirl! Oh, one could never bear
The joyfulness of a sudden start—
So come in little ways, O Spring,
And thrill my being till I sing.

Another Spring

Kay Hoffman

April days have come again
To lift our spirits high.
There is a brand new shade of blue
In the morning sky.

The fragrant scent of blossoms
Drifts o'er the hill and way;
Now daffodils are nodding
Where lately snowflakes lay.

There comes the urge to open wide
The windows in each room
To let in all the fresh, sweet smell
Of April's rare perfume.

The grass is sprouting green again,
Dogwoods are wondrous fair;
And in my neighbor's yard I see
Bright tulips blooming there.

I am so very happy;
My heart can't help but sing.
Our God in loving kindness
Has sent another spring.

Children hold spring so tightly
in their brown fists—
just as grownups, who are
less sure of it,
hold it in their hearts.

—E. B. White

Welcome, Spring!

Mary Ellen Stelling

O Spring, how sweetly you have kissed
Each hill and dale with amethyst!
Every little shrub that stands
Bears flowering blossoms in its hands,

And all the lovely meadow spots
Are knee deep in forget-me-nots.
Across a curving line of hills
March armies of bright daffodils,

And in the dawn I hear again
The gentle sluice of silver rain.
How glad I am to feast my eyes
On springtime's beauty when I rise!

Bravely, This Daffodil

Jean Ravenscroft

Bravely, this daffodil,
Green, wispy, and frail,
Has her creamy face lifted,
Frostbitten and pale.

Though spring's cruel reversals
Have taken their toll,
She fiercely determines
To hold fast her goal.

Undaunted commitment,
God's will for her life,
She blooms where she's planted;
His strength will suffice.

O God, give us courage
And strengthening power
To match the commitment
Of this precious flower.

DAFFODILS
Door County, Wisconsin
Darryl R. Beers Photography

A SLICE OF LIFE

— Edgar A. Guest —

HELLO, TULIPS

Hello, tulips, don't you know
    Stocks today are very low?
You appear so bright and glad;
    Don't you know that trade is bad?
You are just as fair to see
    As you were in times when we

Rolled in money. Tell me how
    You can look so happy now.

Hello, tulips, white and red,
    Gleaming in the garden bed,
Can it be you haven't heard

All the grief which has occurred?
Don't you see the saddened eye
   Of the human passer-by?
By his frowning, can't you tell
   Things have not been going well?

Hello, tulips, in the sun,
   You are lovely, every one.
But I wonder, why don't you
   Wear a sad expression too?
Can it be you fail to see
   Things aren't what they used to be?

This old world is all upset;
   Why don't you begin to fret?

And they answered me: "Hello,
   Nothing's altered that we know.
Warm the sun, and sweet the rain,
   Summer skies are blue again,
Birds are singing, and we nod
   Grateful tulip prayers to God.
Only mortals fret and strive;
   We are glad to be alive."

Edgar A. Guest began his illustrious career in 1895 at the age of fourteen when his work first appeared in the Detroit Free Press. *His column was syndicated in over 300 newspapers, and he became known as "The Poet of the People."*

From My Garden Journal
by Deana Deck

FORSYTHIA

Whether you experience hard winters or mild winters in your hometown, there's nothing that lifts the spirit like the sight of the first early blossoms of the brilliant yellow forsythia. It's a shrub that fairly shouts, "Good-bye winter, hello spring!"

Delicate as it may appear in spring, the forsythia is one tough plant. I once planted a defenseless, little one-gallon specimen beside the driveway of the first house I ever bought. As a new homeowner, I was thrilled to have it mark my boundary. Actually, I was thrilled just to have a boundary to mark; but I formed a strong attachment to that forsythia and carefully nurtured it through its first two years. When I sold the house, I was racked with guilt over abandoning the little plant.

The people who bought the house were not interested in gardens by any stretch of the imagination, and they left the yard and flowers to languish and die—including the lawn, over which I had sweated for hours. When I returned to the city a few years later,

I was appalled at what I saw. Not only was everything dead, it was gone. The house was being torn down and the lot bulldozed to put in an apartment complex. Somehow, though, the heartless developers had overlooked the forsythia. There it stood, barely three feet tall and quite shabby looking with broken limbs dragging the gravel-strewn soil while the bulldozer inched closer every day.

I couldn't stand it. That very night I enlisted the aid of a pal; and together we stole over to the site around midnight with a flashlight, a shovel, and a burlap bag. We dug up the little forsythia, carried it home, and planted it in the dead of night in a hole we had carefully prepared earlier.

This was in late summer; and I nursed the plant through winter, not fully believing it would survive since many large roots had broken off during digging and it had been stressed by neglect to begin with. You can imagine my joy the following March when I looked out one morning and saw the forsythia had bravely popped into bloom. I gave it an extra shot of compost as a reward.

Forsythia is truly one of the most carefree plants I know of. It is not stalked by deadly diseases and fungal infections. No insects or caterpillars seem interested in chewing it to shreds. It grows in just about any type soil and actually thrives in urban conditions. It blooms profusely whether you feed it or not. It can survive drought, hard freezes, wet springs, and hot summers without protest. I have never seen it refuse to bloom. Granted, a late frost can knock back almost a season's worth of buds; but somewhere, down near the bottom of the bush, a few will survive and gamely don their sunshine yellow as best they can.

Even the blossoms seem impervious to damage. I have, on occasion, gone out and brushed a late, surprise dusting of snow off of a blooming forsythia before cutting a few branches to bring indoors. They were none the worse for the experience.

One of the best characteristics of the plant is that it can be forced into bloom as early as January simply by cutting a few branches and sticking them into a vase of water in a sunny spot.

Forsythia is hard to kill; but unlike many other plants of which the same can be said— honeysuckle, for example—it doesn't insist on reproducing itself throughout your yard and that of the neighbors. In fact I've never seen it even attempt to travel, although there are varieties known to take root where their arching branches touch the ground.

The forsythias are fast-growing shrubs, easily propagated by either hard or softwood cuttings, and are known to live for fifty or sixty years in perfect conditions. There are a number of species of forsythia, and all produce yellow flowers in spring before leaves appear. Growers have developed a range of color that extends from pale, pale primrose yellow to vibrant, deep gold.

There is also a Korean shrub marketed as a white forsythia which, although related to forsythia, is actually an *Abeliophyllum distichum*. It blooms about the same time as forsythia and resembles it in appearance, but is much more fragrant.

While forsythia can be sheared to create a formal hedge, leaving the plants alone lets them develop their graceful, arching shape. A plant does not need pruning unless it outgrows its space, but older branches should be thinned out occasionally to encourage vigorous growth. Remove about one third of the oldest wood each year. Because the forsythia's buds form on wood produced the previous summer, it's best to prune immediately after it has ceased flowering in spring.

Sometimes forsythias are pruned to keep them confined to a smaller area. There is a dwarf variety, however, that can be allowed to grow naturally but which will take up much less space. Ideal for those with postage-stamp lawns, Gold Tide only grows to about two feet in height and four feet in width.

One of the most beautiful varieties available today is the *Forsythia x intermedia*, Spring Glory, which is a primrose yellow species that is excellent for forcing in late winter. Northern gardeners will want to seek out the *F. ovata*, Meadowlark, an early blooming and extremely hardy species developed in North and South Dakota. Its buds are hardy to -35° Fahrenheit. Since many species will suffer bud damage at temperatures below -10° Fahrenheit, these are good choices for New England and the upper Midwest.

Each year, I anxiously await those first few early weeks of golden blossoms from my favorite forsythia plant. It has been six years now since my friend and I rescued my little forsythia. It's now a mature beauty that reigns over my spring garden with strong arching branches loaded with heavy blooms. Whenever I catch a glimpse of it in its full spring glory, the word resurrection always comes to mind.

Deana Deck lives in Nashville, Tennessee, where her popular garden column is a regular feature in The Tennessean.

Planting Time

Valorie R. Hornsby

One morning when the sun is bright
And Spring has sprung with all its might,

The corner garden's rich brown dirt
Will beckon me with shameless flirt.

She'll wave her scents of dampened earth,
And I'll comply with avid mirth.

For somewhere deep inside of me,
A farmer lurks to be set free.

I'll sow some seeds and watch them grow,
All lined and pretty in a row.

Yes, somewhere deep inside of me,
There is a need to plant a seed.

TULIP FARM
Willamette Valley, Oregon
Steve Terrill Photography

COLLECTOR'S CORNER

CLOISONNÉ

by Patricia A. Pingry

Many years ago, my long-time neighbor who had taught in mission schools around the world was packing up her household and, once more, moving to a new mission school. Before leaving, she knocked on our door to bid us farewell and presented my mother with a small, varied-colored, metallic box that she had picked up in the Orient and which looked, to the child I was, much like the stained glass windows of our church. Years later, I acquired the box, and I kept it on the dresser as a memento of our neighbor but more as a receptacle for odd, loose buttons and pins that I constantly pick up around the house. At an antique store one day, however, I discovered that my "stained glass" box was actually a piece of cloisonné.

Cloisonné is an ancient method of decoration; the surface of a piece of cloisonné is composed of many various colors of melted enamels separated by thin wires which form the *cloison*, the French word for "cell." Since the chemical composition of enamel is silicon, or glass, cloisonné could be called an arrangement of pieces of colored glass; therefore, it really does have some distant relationship to a stained glass window.

The origin of enameling is unknown, but probably began by melting colored glass on objects to simulate the look of the jewel-encrusted bowls and jewelry of the wealthy. The ancient Greeks decorated gold jewelry with minute quantities of melted blue and white enamels contained by thin gold wire; but the art of enameling blossomed in the early part of the Byzantine civilization in the ninth century B.C. Translucent green, white, red, yellow, purple, and black enamels were applied to backgrounds of gold and silver. Individual pieces were exquisite and tiny—no more than one to two inches across. There are extant book covers that were built up from a number of panels, each composed of miniature enamels that shine like jewels against their gold backgrounds. The earliest enamels that have been unearthed are jewelry from the Mycenaean period of Greece, or around the thirteenth century B.C.

Although cloisonné probably developed in the ancient civilizations of Greece and Europe, Chinese and Japanese craftsmen perfected the process as an art form. Oriental cloisonné pieces make a safe investment for collectors since most pieces available are products of the nineteenth and twentieth centuries; thus the value that comes with age is not a factor. The rare specimens from the very early periods are safely ensconced in museums, so don't count on finding a bowl from the Ming or Ch'ing dynasties at your favorite antique store.

The process of making cloisonné is, to me, so complex that I think all pieces of cloisonné are worthy of admiration. Since silicon glass is colorless, various metallic oxides are added to produce rich colors. For instance, the addition of copper produces green and turquoise, arsenic makes white, manganese turns purple, and cobalt creates a rich blue. Once a design and the colors are chosen, cloisonné artists begin their project by hammering out a metallic base in the shape of the finished piece; but the metal they choose must meet several criteria. It must be pliable enough so that it can be hammered into the shape of a bowl, plate, vase, or a piece of jewelry; but the melting temperature of the metal must be higher than 850° Celsius, the temperature at which the enamels fuse. Chemists know that gold meets these criteria best, followed by silver; but these metals have the problem of cost. Since gold and silver have always been rare, these metals were seldom used as a base for cloisonné except for the very rich or royalty. Other than gold or silver, the best metals for a base are copper and the alloys of bronze and brass. The wires that contain the enamels, however, are often of gold or silver or the less expensive copper.

If you are looking for cloisonné, you should

know that there are two crafts similar in appearance. These also use melted enamels, but employ different methods of keeping the melted enamels separated. In the first, *champlevé*, the artisan carves cells out of a solid metal, thereby containing the different colors as they melt; and in the second, *repoussé*, the craftsperson, in hammering out the base from a metal sheet, forms small depressions to contain the colors.

In cloisonné, the enamel colors are separated by the tiny wires that are bent and soldered to the base metal. Often these wires are gold, and cloisonné offers the most economical way to use the gold (in wires rather than as a base). Another function of the wires is to provide a structural anchor and relieve stress on the metals. Experts tell me that enamel and the metal of the base do not make a permanent union; different rates of expansion and contraction could make the enamel pop off or at least crack without these wires to relieve the metal stress.

CLOISONNÉ ELEPHANTS. Superstock.

In the fifteenth century, the artisans of Limoges, France, began experimenting with another way of containing the colors. They painted the enamels directly on copper, which sounds like an easier way to me, but it took two hundred more years to perfect this method. In Limoges enameling, the artisan builds up several layers of painted enamel with firings after each layer.

The value of a cloisonné piece depends upon several factors. First and foremost, like any other collectible, the collector must fall in love with the object. This was probably the case in 1974 when, at a sale at Sotheby's, a Ming statue that had just been appraised at $3,500 fetched a bid of $29,000 from a collector. Don't count on finding such a bargain at your local second-hand store; however, there are tales of collectors stumbling upon pieces that later were appraised for as much as ten times what they paid. If you do run across a piece of cloisonné that you love and want to evaluate its worth, look at the wires and determine if they are gold or silver, which would add to the value. Also, the more wire and enamel work, the higher its worth. In addition, the value of the cloisonné depends upon how expertly, how intricately, and how artistically the design is rendered. In rare cases, the base material itself might be valuable; turn the piece over and check for gold or silver.

And my box? It is worth a little more money than I thought it was, but it certainly will not be sought after by serious collectors. My "stained glass" box knows its place in life and serves its function by sitting on my dresser holding lost buttons, tiny safety pins from the dry cleaners, and stray pennies picked up around the house. But that box is also my connection to the past. It is an ever-present reminder of a next-door neighbor from my childhood, and it's an example of an ancient art crafted by an unknown artisan before I was ever born.

An avid book collector, Patricia A. Pingry is always searching for another first edition to add to her extensive library, which will be complete when she obtains an autographed copy of her favorite book, Louisa May Alcott's Little Women.

My Garden Is a Pleasant Place

Louise Driscoll

My garden is a pleasant place
Of sun glory and leaf grace.
There is an ancient cherry tree
Where yellow warblers sing to me;
And an old grape arbor where
A robin builds her nest; and there
Above the lima beans and peas
She croons her little melodies,
Her blue eggs hidden in the green
Fastness of that leafy screen.

Here are striped zinnias that bees
Fly far to visit and sweet peas
Like little butterflies newborn.
And over by the tasseled corn
Are sunflowers and hollyhocks,
And pink and yellow four-o'clocks.
Here are hummingbirds that come
To seek the tall delphinium—
Songless bird and scentless flower
Communing in a golden hour.

There is no blue like the blue cup
The tall delphinium holds up—
Not sky, nor distant hill, nor sea,
Sapphire, nor lapis lazuli.

My lilac trees are old and tall;
I cannot reach their blooms at all.
They send their perfume over trees
And roofs and streets to find the bees.

I wish some power would touch my ear
With magic touch and make me hear
What all the blossoms say; and so
I might know what the winged things know.
I'd hear the sunflower's mellow pipe,
"Goldfinch, goldfinch, my seeds are ripe!"
I'd hear the pale wisteria sing,
"Moon moth, moon moth, I'm blossoming!"

I'd hear the evening primrose cry,
"O firefly! Come, firefly!"
And I would learn the jeweled word
The ruby-throated hummingbird
Drops into cups of larkspur blue,
And I could sing them all for you!

My garden is a pleasant place
Of moon glory and wind grace.
O friend, wherever you may be,
Will you not come to visit me?
Over fields and streams and hills,
I'll pipe like yellow daffodils;
And every little wind that blows
Shall take my message as it goes.
A heart may travel very far
To come where its desires are.
Oh, may some power touch my ear,
And grant me grace, and make you hear!

WILD PHLOX. Mt. Hood National Forest, Oregon. Steve Terrill Photography.

April Rain

Robert Loveman

It is not raining rain to me,
    It's raining daffodils;
In every dimpled drop I see
    Wildflowers on the hills.
The clouds of gray engulf the day
    And overwhelm the town;
It is not raining rain to me,
    It's raining roses down.

It is not raining rain to me,
    But fields of clover bloom
Where every buccaneering bee
    May find a bed and room.
A health unto the happy!
    A fig for him who frets!
It is not raining rain to me,
    It's raining violets.

The unique perspective of Russ Flint's artistic style has made him a favorite of **Ideals** *readers for many years. A resident of California and father of four, Russ Flint has illustrated a children's Bible and many other books.*

*"Only a child can catch a
raindrop or see any value
in puddles."*

—D. F. Gill

Rhythm of the Rain

Joy Belle Burgess

Oh, now I hear the music
Of the happy, falling rain
That tinkles like a million bells
Upon my windowpane
And beats its syncopation
In a rooftop roundelay
With all the rousing rhythm
Of a drum on marching day.

And lo, I hear the raindrops
As they fall among the trees
And whisper through the branches
All their softest litanies.
They play upon their harp strings
As they drop from leaf to leaf
With a faint, exquisite music
Only raindrops can achieve.

And how I love the rhythms
As they fall upon my ear
Along the path and garden
In their melody of cheer
With such a lively tempo
And melodious refrain.
Oh, see the merry tulips
Now dancing in the rain!

WALKIN' IN THE RAIN
Boise, Idaho
Mark W. Lisk/F-Stock

Family Recipes

Favorite Recipes from the Ideals Family of Readers

AUNT DOT'S CARROT CAKE

Preheat oven to 350° F. In a large bowl, sift together 2 cups all-purpose flour, 2 teaspoons baking powder, 2 teaspoons baking soda, ½ teaspoon salt, 2 teaspoons cinnamon, and 2 cups granulated sugar. Stir in ½ cup vegetable oil, 4 beaten eggs, and 2 cups grated carrots; mix well. Add 1 cup drained, crushed pineapple; ½ cup flaked coconut; and ½ cup chopped walnuts. Mix well. Spoon batter into three greased and floured, 8-inch round cake pans. Bake 30 to 35 minutes. Remove from oven and cool in pans 10 minutes; remove from pans to wire racks and cool completely.

In a large bowl, combine ½ cup softened margarine, one 8-ounce package softened cream cheese, and 1 teaspoon vanilla. Slowly add 1 pound sifted powdered sugar. Mix well. Spread frosting between cake layers and on top and sides.

Barb Marshall
Pickerington, Ohio

OLD TOWN POUND CAKE

Preheat oven to 325° F. In a medium bowl, sift together 3 cups all-purpose flour, ½ teaspoon baking powder, and ½ teaspoon salt. Set aside. In a medium bowl, cream 1 cup softened butter and ½ cup vegetable oil with 3 cups granulated sugar until light and fluffy. Add 1 cup buttermilk and 2 teaspoons vanilla. Slowly add flour mixture and mix well. Beat 6 eggs and fold into batter. Pour batter into a greased and floured 10-inch tube pan. Bake 1 hour and 20 minutes.

To make a chocolate pound cake, add one 12-ounce bag melted semisweet chocolate chips to batter.

Fay P. Godwin
Chester, Virginia

FRENCH PASTRY CHOCOLATE CAKE

Preheat oven to 350° F. In a small bowl, add ¾ cup boiling water to ½ cup cocoa; stir and set aside. In a medium bowl, sift 2 cups cake flour, ½ teaspoon baking soda, and 1 teaspoon baking powder. Set aside. In a large bowl, cream ½ cup butter or shortening with 2 cups granulated sugar. Beat in 3 egg yolks and ½ cup sour cream. Add cocoa mixture. Slowly add flour mixture; mix well. Beat 3 egg whites until stiff but not dry and fold into batter. Pour batter into two greased and floured, 8-inch round cake pans. Bake 35 to 40 minutes.

In a double boiler, melt 1 cup semisweet chocolate chips with 2 tablespoons butter over hot (not boiling) water. Remove from heat. Add 3 tablespoons warm milk and 1 teaspoon vanilla. Slowly add 1 cup sifted powdered sugar. Beat until smooth and of spreading consistency. Spread frosting on cake.

Mrs. John Swanson
Mishawaka, Indiana

RED VELVET CAKE

Preheat oven to 350° F. In a large bowl, combine 2½ cups cake flour and 1 teaspoon salt; set aside. In a large bowl, cream ½ cup shortening with 1½ cups granulated sugar until light and fluffy. Beat in 2 eggs. Stir in 2 tablespoons unsweetened cocoa and ½ cup buttermilk. Add flour mixture alternately with an additional ½ cup buttermilk and 1 teaspoon vanilla, mixing thoroughly after each addition. Dissolve 1 teaspoon baking soda in 1 tablespoon white vinegar; add to batter. Add 2 ounces red food coloring and mix well. Pour batter into two greased and floured, 9-inch round cake pans. Bake 30 minutes. Remove from oven and cool in pans 10 minutes; remove from pans to wire racks and cool completely.

In a small saucepan, combine ¼ cup all-purpose flour and 1½ cups milk. Place over medium heat, stirring constantly until mixture is thick. Remove from heat and set aside to cool. In a large bowl, beat 1 cup granulated sugar and 1 cup shortening with an electric mixer until thick and fluffy. Beating at high speed, add the cooled flour mixture one spoonful at a time. Continue beating 5 to 7 minutes or until frosting is thick. Stir in 1 teaspoon vanilla. Spread frosting between cake layers and on top and sides.

Dorothy Baur
Phoenix, Arizona

Editor's Note: Please send us your best-loved recipes! Mail a typed copy of the recipe along with your name, address, and telephone number to Ideals magazine, ATTN: Recipes, P.O. Box 305300, Nashville, Tennessee 37230. We will pay $10 for each recipe used. Recipes cannot be returned.

SUNDAY MORNING WAKE-UP CALL!

Molly Lemmons

"Fresh and hot,
Right out of the pot,
The best you ever got!
They shine your teeth,
They curl your hair,
They make you feel
Like a millionaire!

Now who wants the first one?"

These are the immortal words of our daddy, who all of our young lives was the self-appointed chef on Sunday mornings. Pancakes were his specialty, and he would call us all to breakfast with this rhyme he had used as a child calling passers-by to his corner hamburger stand. We all patiently had to wait our turn for the next batch because a large family in a one-bathroom house had to rotate shifts of eating, bathing, and getting ready for church services.

The familiar "wake-up" call would rouse us all, except Mother. Nobody knew when she had gotten up, or if in fact she had ever even gone to bed! Not a one of us children, and there were five of us, remembers Mother ever being in bed. When we got up, we would find our shoes polished and our dresses pressed and laid out with matching ribbons, socks, and clean underwear. The Sunday suits of our brother and daddy would be fresh from the cleaners and laid out on the bed. The dining room table would be set for Sunday dinner, and there would be extra places set in case someone wanted to come home with us.

The roast would be in the oven, vegetables

on the stove, salads and desserts in the refrigerator, and rolls rising on the countertops. And on Easter Sunday, fresh flowers in our best crystal vase would grace the table. Somewhere in between all of this, Mother dressed for church and had herself ready before we ever heard Daddy's "wake-up call" ringing from the kitchen.

Daddy would take each of our orders for the number of pancakes we wanted. After eating them at the breakfast nook, we would clear the table, do the dishes, and shower and dress for worship. By some miracle, we would all be ready to leave the house just in time for Sunday

SUNDAY MORNING BREAKFAST. Archive Photos.

School and church! The last one of us out the door would check to be sure the door was left unlocked in case a neighbor got home before we did and needed to borrow something. It seems we were always loaning ice.

Today, my parents' old pancake grill is still stored in its place of honor. Its once-shiny surface is now totally black, but there will never be any attempt to scrub off all of those memories. The very sight of it brings to my mind the vision of my dear daddy standing at the stove and flipping pancakes while he whistled.

I can still hear the whistling; and as it stops, a booming voice arouses me from pleasant dreams:

> *"Fresh and hot,*
> *Right out of the pot,*
> *The best you ever got!*
> *They shine your teeth,*
> *They curl your hair,*
> *They make you feel*
> *Like a millionaire!*
>
> *Now who wants the first one?"*

April's Acres

Lon Myruski

When Spring arrives, it styles the land
    In verdant, vogue attire
With winsome scenes woven everywhere;
    Spring artisans conspire.
For wearied hearts of wintertime,
    It's soothing to the soul
To wander April's acres
    And view its fashion show.

The pastures sport new grassy shirts;
    They lie so smartly dressed
And shimmer in the morning sun
    Still in their dewy vests.
And cornfields plowed for planting soon
    Wear richly furrowed stoles
That wind 'cross April's acres
    O'er rolling hills and knolls.

The woodlands stretch their budding limbs
    To meet the sun's embrace
As oak and maple, ash and elm
    Display their new green lace.
And roadsides don a necklace made
    Of countless dandelions,
Arraying April's acres
    In wondrous spring design.

Then dusk descends to drape its cloak
    Of purple velveteen
Upon the distant mountaintops
    So ancient, so pristine.
And somewhere from the darkness
    Spring peepers serenade
To honor April's acres
    And all that God has made.

Readers' Forum

Meet Our Ideals Readers and Their Families

ATTENTION *IDEALS* READERS: The *Ideals* editors are looking for Favorite Easter Memories for the magazine. Please send a typed description of your favorite memory to: Favorite Memories, c/o Editorial Department, Ideals Publications Inc., P.O. Box 305300, Nashville, Tennessee 37230.

Have you been to a special festival or county fair in your area that was especially memorable? We'd like to hear about it. Please send a typed description to: Celebrations, c/o Editorial Department, Ideals Publications Inc., P.O. Box 305300, Nashville, Tennessee 37230.

FAITH DUPUIS of Kennett Square, Pennsylvania, says about 120 aunts, uncles, and cousins are invited to her family's annual Easter egg hunt, which continues a fifty-year family tradition. Pictured here are family members Danielle Burch (left) of Forest, Virginia; Marissa DiMarco (center) of Voorhees, New Jersey; and Faith's daughter Natalie Dupuis (right).

Faith remembers spending hours reading *Ideals* as a child. Now she shares the magazine with her sisters because *Ideals* reminds her of a little "piece of home."

CHERYL AND PETER DEKOVA sent us this picture of their favorite Easter bunny. Katelyn, age two, loves to visit the local flower market in Vancouver, British Columbia, where she and her parents live. Last year, Katelyn donned her bunny suit to wish everyone a happy Easter!

One of Cheryl's favorite Easter traditions is sharing *Ideals*. Her father read *Ideals* poetry to her when she was a child, and she decided to carry on the family tradition. Cheryl's other hobbies include flower arranging, gardening, and playing the piano with Katelyn.

ESTHER HAARSTAD, who lives in Golden Valley, Minnesota, sent us this photo of her great-granddaughter Casey, her little ray of sunshine. Casey is the daughter of Paul and Teri Haarstad of Chaska, Minnesota. This picture was taken last Easter when Casey was one year old.

In honor of Casey, Esther wrote the poem below:

TO CASEY
Esther Haarstad

Let me tell you, little charmer
Why my love for you grows warmer.
When I look into your eyes,
I see the blue of summer skies.

Your cheeks glow with the glow of spring,
Your lips the color tulips bring.
Your little nose is sweet and fair;
The sun lights up your auburn hair.

Your soft and tender outstretched arms
Hold me captive to your charms.
You seem to be in pensive mood;
Do you mind if I intrude?

May angels guard you all your days
And Jesus lead you in His ways
Until we reach the heavenly shore
Where loved ones live forevermore.

THANK YOU Faith Dupuis, Cheryl and Peter DeKova, and Esther Haarstad for sharing with *Ideals*. We hope to hear from other readers who would like to share photos and stories with the *Ideals* family. Please include a self-addressed, stamped envelope if you would like the photos returned. Keep your original photographs for safekeeping and send duplicate photos along with your name, address, and telephone number to:

READERS' FORUM
IDEALS PUBLICATIONS INC.
P.O. BOX 305300
NASHVILLE, TENNESSEE 37230

Publisher, Patricia A. Pingry
Editor, Lisa C. Ragan
Copy Editor, Michelle Prater Burke
Electronic Prepress Manager, Amilyn K. Lanning
Editorial Intern, Laura K. Griffis
Contributing Editors, Lansing Christman, Deana Deck, Russ Flint, Pamela Kennedy, Patrick McRae, Mary Skarmeas, Nancy Skarmeas

ACKNOWLEDGMENTS

HELLO, TULIPS from *LIFE'S HIGHWAY* by Edgar A. Guest, copyright ©1933 by The Reilly & Lee Co. Used by permission of the author's estate. MORNING SONG from *IN BEAUTY'S PRESENCE* by Isla Paschal Richardson, copyright ©1952 by Bruce Humphries, Inc. Reprinted courtesy of Branden Publishing Company, Boston. APRIL from *THE STILLMEADOW ROAD* by Gladys Taber, copyright ©1962 by Gladys Taber. Reprinted by permission of Brandt & Brandt Literary Agents, Inc. Our sincere thanks to the following authors whom we were unable to contact: Nancy S. Boston for AN EASTER OFFERING, Louise Driscoll for MY GARDEN IS A PLEASANT PLACE, and Ethel Bruce Pittman for COME GENTLY, SPRING.

The Lamb

William Blake

Little lamb, who made thee?
Dost thou know who made thee,
Gave thee life and bade thee feed
By the stream and o'er the mead;
Gave thee clothing of delight,
Softest clothing, woolly, bright;
Gave thee such a tender voice,
Making all the vales rejoice?
    Little lamb, who made thee?
    Dost thou know who made thee?

Little lamb, I'll tell thee;
Little lamb, I'll tell thee.
He is called by thy name,
For He calls Himself a Lamb;
He is meek and He is mild;
He became a little child.
I a child and thou a lamb,
We are called by His name.
    Little lamb, God bless thee!
    Little lamb, God bless thee!